Be Kind

Dona Herweck Rice

Library of Congress Cataloging-in-Publication Data

Names: Rice, Dona, author.
Title: Be kind / Dona Herweck Rice.
Description: Huntington Beach : Teacher Created Materials, 2018. |
Identifiers: LCCN 2018020219 (print) | LCCN 2018021745 (ebook) | ISBN 9781493898879 | ISBN 9781493898138 (pbk.)
Subjects: LCSH: Kindness–Juvenile literature.
Classification: LCC BJ1533.K5 (ebook) | LCC BJ1533.K5 R53 2018 (print) | DDC 177/.7–dc23
LC record available at https://lccn.loc.gov/2018020219

Publishing Credits

Rachelle Cracchiolo, M.S.Ed., *Publisher*
Conni Medina, M.A.Ed., *Managing Editor*
Nika Fabienke, Ed.D., *Content Director*
Véronique Bos, *Creative Director*
Shaun N. Bernadou, *Art Director*
Carol Huey-Gatewood, M.A.Ed., *Editor*
Valerie Morales, *Associate Editor*
Courtney Roberson, *Senior Graphic Designer*

Image Credits: All images from iStock and/or Shutterstock.

Teacher Created Materials
5301 Oceanus Drive
Huntington Beach, CA 92649-1030
www.tcmpub.com

ISBN 978-1-4938-9813-8

Printed in China
51497

Be  with a  .

kind

pet

Be  with a  .

kind baby

Be  with a  .

kind librarian

Be  with a  .

kind teacher

Be  with a  .

kind server

Be kind with a clerk.

Be  kind with a  driver.

Be  with a  .

kind

team

Be  with a  .

kind friend

Be  with a  .

kind

family

High-Frequency Words

a

be

with